Bighorn Sheep

By JoAnn Early Macken

Reading Consultant: Jeanne Clidas, Ph.D.
Director, Roberts Wesleyan College Literacy Clinic

WEEKLY READER®
PUBLISHING

Please visit our web site at **www.garethstevens.com**.
For a free catalog describing our list of high-quality books,
call 1-877-542-2595 (USA) or 1-800-387-3178 (Canada).
Our fax: 1-877-542-2596

Library of Congress Cataloging-in-Publication Data

Macken, JoAnn Early, 1953–
     Bighorn sheep / by JoAnn Early Macken.
        p. cm. — (Animals that live in the mountains)
     Includes bibliographical references and index.
     ISBN-10: 1-4339-2409-9   ISBN-13: 978-1-4339-2409-5 (lib. bdg.)
     ISBN-10: 1-4339-2492-7   ISBN-13: 978-1-4339-2492-7 (soft cover)
     1. Bighorn sheep—Juvenile literature. I. Title.
QL737.U53M215   2009
599.649'7–dc22
                                            2009000100

This edition first published in 2010 by
Weekly Reader® Books
An Imprint of Gareth Stevens Publishing
1 Reader's Digest Road
Pleasantville, NY 10570-7000 USA

Copyright © 2010 by Gareth Stevens, Inc.

Executive Managing Editor: Lisa M. Herrington
Senior Editor: Barbara Bakowski
Project Management: Spooky Cheetah Press
Cover Designers: Jennifer Ryder-Talbot and Studio Montage
Production: Studio Montage
Library Consultant: Carl Harvey, Library Media Specialist, Noblesville, Indiana

Photo credits: Cover, pp. 1, 7, 13 Shutterstock; p. 5 © Alan and Sandy Carey; pp. 9, 11, 17 © Michael H. Francis; pp. 15, 19, 21 © Tom and Pat Leeson

Printed in the United States of America

1 2 3 4 5 6 7 8 9 14 13 12 11 10 09

Table of Contents

Food for a Bighorn Sheep. 4

Staying Safe 8

Time for a Change 18

Glossary. 22

For More Information 23

Index 24

Boldface words appear in the glossary.

Food for a Bighorn Sheep

A bighorn sheep can stand soon after it is born. A baby, or **lamb**, can walk in a few hours. Soon it can run and jump. A female sheep, or **ewe**, feeds her lamb milk.

lamb

In a few months, lambs eat grass. Sheep swallow their food in quick bites. Later, they bring it up to chew it. Then they swallow it again.

Staying Safe

Ewes and lambs stay in a group. Lambs play with each other. Males, or **rams**, stay in their own group. One sheep watches out for danger.

Bighorns can see far away. If a ewe sees danger, she stamps her foot. If a ram sees danger, he **snorts**. The group runs down the mountain.

Bighorns are good at climbing. Their feet do not slip. Sheep leap from rock to rock.

13

A bighorn sheep's horns keep growing. A ram's horns grow back and down. They can curl into circles. A ewe's horns are not as thick as a ram's. They do not curl into circles.

15

Rams fight with their horns.
Crash! They slam into
each other!

Time for a Change

In winter, snow can cover the grass. Sheep scrape away the snow. A group may move to a place with less snow.

Bighorns grow heavy coats for winter. In spring, they **shed**, or lose, some hair. They look for green grass to eat.

Fast Facts

Height	about 3 feet (1 meter) at the shoulder
Length	about 5 feet (2 meters) nose to tail
Weight	Males: about 275 pounds (125 kilograms) Females: about 150 pounds (68 kilograms)
Diet	grasses and leaves
Average life span	up to 20 years

Glossary

ewe: a female sheep

lamb: a baby sheep

rams: male sheep

shed: to lose hair, skin, horn, or feathers

snorts: makes a sound by blowing air out through the nose

For More Information

Books

I Live in the Mountains. Where I Live (series). Gini Holland (Gareth Stevens, 2004)

Mountains. Habitats (series). Fran Howard (Abdo Publishing, 2006)

Web Sites

Bighorn Sheep
www.nhptv.org/Natureworks/bighornsheep.htm
See lots of photos, and read all about bighorn sheep.

Bighorn Sheep
www.enchantedlearning.com/subjects/mammals/sheep/Bighornsheep.shtml
Color a diagram of a bighorn sheep.

Publisher's note to educators and parents: Our editors have carefully reviewed these web sites to ensure that they are suitable for children. Many web sites change frequently, however, and we cannot guarantee that a site's future contents will continue to meet our high standards of quality and educational value. Be advised that children should be closely supervised whenever they access the Internet.

Index

climbing 12

danger 8, 10

ewes 4, 8, 10, 14

fighting 16

food 4, 6, 20

grass 6, 18, 20

hair 20

horns 14, 16

jumping 4, 12

lambs 4, 6, 8

playing 8

rams 8, 10, 14, 16

running 4, 10

winter 18, 20

About the Author

JoAnn Early Macken is the author of two rhyming picture books, *Sing-Along Song* and *Cats on Judy*, and more than 80 nonfiction books for children. Her poems have appeared in several children's magazines. She lives in Wisconsin with her husband and their two sons.